〔日〕吉河 功 / 摄
孙来庆 / 汉译
张辰毅 / 英译

苏州耦园之美

苏州大学出版社

图书在版编目(CIP)数据

苏州耦园之美：日、汉、英/(日)吉河 功 摄，孙来庆汉译，张辰毅英译．—苏州：苏州大学出版社，2015.10
ISBN 978-7-5672-1344-9

Ⅰ.①苏… Ⅱ.①吉…②孙…③张… Ⅲ.①古典园林—苏州市—摄影集 Ⅳ.①K928.73-64

中国版本图书馆 CIP 数据核字(2015)第 241452 号

书　　名：苏州耦园之美

作　　者：〔日〕吉河 功/摄
孙来庆/汉译
张辰毅/英译
责任编辑：汤定军
策划编辑：汤定军
装帧设计：吴 钰

出版发行：苏州大学出版社(Soochow University Press)
社　　址：苏州市十梓街 1 号　邮编：215006
印　　装：苏州工业园区美柯乐制版印务有限责任公司
网　　址：www.sudapress.com
E - mail：tangdingjun@suda.edu.cn
邮购热线：0512-67480030
销售热线：0512-65225020

开　　本：700mm×1000mm　1/16　印张：6.25　字数：30 千
版　　次：2015 年 10 月第 1 版
印　　次：2015 年 10 月第 1 次印刷
书　　号：ISBN 978-7-5672-1344-9
定　　价：48.00 元

前 言

蘇州城の東北、小新橋巷にある耦園は、蘇州園林の中でも特別の樂しさを持つ世界文化遺産指定の名園である。

全園は三つの部分に分かれており、中央の旧住居部を挟んで東花園と西花園がある。最も古いのは東花園中央にある規模の大きな黄石築山であって、清代雍正年間(1723～1735)に作られた渉園の遺跡といわれている。

園林建築もまた特色に満ちたもので、屋根先にある独特の飾りは優雅で美しい。

廊にある漏窓も風雅そのものである。また東花園が黄石を主としているのに対して、西花園は太湖石の築山に特色を見せており、正に耦園(耦は偶に通ずる)、すなわち夫婦の園に相応しい佇まいといえよう。

東花園の東北にある雙照楼は、私の主催する日本庭園研究会が1983年に初訪中した時、蘇州園林学会と学術交流会を開いた思い出の場所でもある。

それ以来、何度も足を運んで撮影した成果がこの写真集に凝縮されているものと信じている。

吉河 功

前 言

位于苏州城东北处小新桥巷里的耦园，即便在苏州园林中，也是一处特别令人欣慰的被世界文化遗产所指定的名园。

全园分为三个部分，位于中部的旧居住部把东花园和西花园隔开。东花园中央的一处大规模的黄石假山非常古老，相传是建造于清代雍正年间(1723—1735)的名为“涉园”的遗迹。

耦园的园林建筑也充满了特色，飞檐的装饰既优雅又美观，走廊墙面上的漏窗风雅至极。与东花园黄石假山相比，西花园可以让人欣赏到太湖石假山的特色。这真是名副其实的耦园(耦通偶意)，即可以说，耦园呈现出与夫妻园相般配的形态。

在东花园东北部的双照楼，是我组织的日本庭园研究会在1983年初次访华时，与苏州园林学会举办过学术交流会的令人回忆的场所。

我相信，自那以来我无数次地来到耦园，举起相机的摄影成果都浓缩在这本写真集里了。

吉河 功

Preface

Located in a small lane named the Xiaoxingqiao Lane (Little New Bridge Lane) in the northeastern part of Suzhou City, the Couple's Retreat Garden, even among other classical Suzhou gardens, is a place with special comfort and enjoyment as a world heritage site.

It is divided into three parts, with its East Garden and West Garden separated by the previous residential core in the middle. At the center of the East Garden lies an ancient, large-scale yellow-stone rockery, regarded as a historic site from the Sheyuan Garden dated back to between 1723 and 1735 in the Qing Dynasty.

Its garden buildings are embodied with distinctive characteristics: the overhanging eaves with elegant decorations and the corridor walls with graceful lattice-framed windows. Coupled with the yellow-stone rockery in the East Garden, the rockery in the West Garden heaped with stones from Taihu Lake sports its own style, so such purposeful designing in couple is totally fit with the implication of the name of garden.

The Sun and Moon Tower in the East Garden is a place full of beautiful memories where a conference was held in 1983 between the Society of Suzhou Gardens and the Society of Japanese Gardens, the first visit of the Society I arranged to China.

I believe, the essence of the photos I have taken during my innumerable visits here after that meeting is condensed in this photo album.

Yoshikawa Isao

目 次　目 录　CONTENTS

東花園

东花园

East Garden

東花園の円洞門
东花园的圆洞门
round-shaped doorframe in the East Garden

園門と廊
园门和走廊
round-shaped doorframe and corridor

屋根の塑像
飞檐的塑像
decoration on the overhanging eave

石笋と太湖石
石笋和太湖石
stalagmites and Taihu Lake stones

樨廊　　樨廊(せいろう)は東花園の西側にある廊で、その北庭から、南庭の魁星閣まで続ている。
樨廊　　樨廊是一条在东花园西侧的走廊,它从北部庭园一直延伸到南部庭园的魁星阁。
osmanthus corridor, a corridor in the west of the East Garden stretching from north to south till the Kuixing Pavilion

樨廊　　樨廊は東側の筠廊(いんろう)とは異なった様式で、美しい漏窓の連なる景に特色がある。

樨廊　　樨廊与东侧的筠廊的样式迥异,其特色在于一个接连一个的漂亮的漏窗。

osmanthus corridor, different from the Yunlang Corridor in the east, specialized in its elegant lattice-framed windows in a row

樨廊西側
樨廊西侧
west to the osmanthus corridor

円形漏窓　円形漏窓細部
圆形漏窗及其特写
round-shaped lattice-framed window and its close-up feature

廊と漏窓
走廊和漏窗
corridor and lattice-framed windows

漏窓秋景
漏窗秋景
autumn view through the lattice-framed window

漏窓
漏窗
lattice-framed window

漏窓
漏窗
lattice-framed window

樨廊南側
樨廊南側
south to the osmanthus corridor

廊の屋根飾り
走廊的飞檐装饰
decoration on the overhanging eave of the corridor

山水間全景　　山水間は南庭の中心建築で大半が水上に建てられている。

山水间全景　　山水间是南部庭园的主建筑，其大部分建造在水面之上。

general view of the Amongst the Mountain and Water Hall, the main building in the south of the garden mostly built upon the water surface

山水間内景　　山水間の扁額は康熙皇帝に愛された書家沈筌(しんせん)の名筆である。

山水间内景　　山水间的匾额是康熙皇帝所喜爱的书法家沈筌书写的。

inside view of the Amongst the Mountain and Water Hall, the handwriting on the plague above written by Shen Quan, a calligrapher favored by Emperor Kangxi in the Qing Dynasty

山水間屋根裏
山水间内屋顶
ceiling of the Amongst the Mountain and Water Hall

山水間南側　山水間南側にある飾り彫刻を「落地罩(らくちとう)」と言い、松竹梅が彫られている。蘇州園林中でも最も優れた作として知られる。

山水间南侧　山水间南侧的装饰性雕刻叫作"落地罩",上面雕刻着松竹梅,在苏州园林中是最优美的雕刻作品。

south of the Amongst the Mountain and Water Hall, the decorative wood carving, called "wrap to floor", with bamboos and pines, the best wood-carving masterpiece in the classical gardens in Suzhou

魁星閣　　山水間の背もたれを通して魁星閣を望む。この背もたれを鵝頚椅(がけいい)と言う。

魁星阁　　通过山水间的靠背眺望魁星阁,这种靠背也叫“吴王靠”。

Kuixing Pavilion, from a distant view upon the backrest of the Amongst the Mountain and Water Hall, this style of the backrest also named “King Wu's Style”

山水間木彫細部 鵝頚椅の蓮華彫刻
山水间木雕特写以及吴王靠莲花雕刻
close-up feature of woodcarving in the Amongst the Mountain and Water Hall and close-up feature of lotus-shaped woodcarving of the King-Wu's-Style backrest

藤花と山水間

紫藤花和山水间

wisteria and the Amongst the Mountain and Water Hall

池景　　山水間より北側の受月池を望む。
池景　　从山水间北望受月池。
a scene of the Moon-Loving Pool, to the north of the Amongst the Mountain and Water Hall

山水間妻飾り　　耦園にある数々の塑像は蘇州園林中でも優れた作として知られている。
山水间山墙上部塑像　　耦园里的众多的塑像，即使在苏州园林中也都是卓越的作品。
sculpture decoration on the upper wall of the Amongst the Mountain and Water Hall, along with many others in the garden, ranking top in the classical gardens in Suzhou

山水間屋根飾り
山水间飞檐装饰
decoration on the overhanging eave of the Amongst the Mountain and Water Hall

聴櫓楼と魁星閣　奥にある聴櫓楼上層に上るには右の魁星閣上層の廊から渡る様式である。
听橹楼和魁星阁　要登上左边的听橹楼的二楼，必须从魁星阁的二楼的走廊过去。
Listening to Sculling Boats Tower and Kuixing Pavilion,
the only access to the second floor of Listening to Sculling Boats Tower on the left is through the second-floor corridor of the Kuixing Pavilion

聽櫓楼(左)と魁星閣(右)
听橹楼(左)和魁星阁(右)
Listening to Sculling Boats Tower (left) and Kuixing Pavilion (right)

聽櫓楼内景
听橹楼内景
inside view of the Listening to Sculling Boats Tower

便静宧　　「便静宧(べんせいかん)」とは静かな小室を意味している。
便静宧　　所谓“便静宧”,意为安静的小屋。
Taoism Practicing House, a place for peace and mindfulness

魁星閣花窓
魁星阁花窗
lattice-framed windows of the Kuixing Pavilion

魁星閣屋根飾り
魁星阁飞檐装饰
decoration on the overhanging eave of the Kuixing Pavilion

筼廊と吾愛亭
筼廊和吾爱亭
Yunlang Corridor (Bamboo Grove Corridor) and My Lovable Pavilion

蝙蝠(こうもり)は吉祥の象徴であり、
園林には必ず用いられる意匠である。
蝙蝠是吉祥的象征,这是园林必用的构思。
bats as a symbol of good luck essential in garden designing

吾愛亭と同亭の妻飾り
吾爱亭以及山墙上部塑像
My Lovable Pavillion and sculpture decoration on the upper wall

黄石と竹景
黄石和竹景
a scene of yellow stones and bamboos

廊と漏窓　　筠廊(いんろう)の中央部を西から見た景。漏窓が見事な景観を作り出している。右手は吾愛亭。

走廊和漏窗　　从西面可见筠廊中央的景色,漏窗形成了漂亮的景观。右侧是吾爱亭。

corridor and lattice-framed windows, a view of the central part of the Yunlang Corridor from the west, with the decoration of lattice-framed windows as a highlight, My Lovable Pavillion lying to the right

南部園景
南部园景
a scene in the south of the garden

曲橋「宛虹杠」
曲桥“宛虹杠”
a zigzag bridge, Rainbow-like Bridge

石柱と石刻
石柱和石刻
stone pillars and stone-carving

曲橋と池景
曲桥和池景
a scene of the zigzag bridge and the pool

東部園路
东部园路
pathway in the east of the garden

東花園東側にある篔廊は屈曲が見事で、大部分が風の通る空廊になっている。
位于东花园东侧的篔廊以弯曲为特色，大部分是通风空廊。
Yunlang Corridor, with its winding shape as a distinctive feature, lying in the east of the East Garden, mostly open for good ventilation

篔廊と扁額
篔廊以及匾额
Yunlang Corridor and its plaque

瓶形洞門
瓶形洞门
vase-shaped doorframe

黄石築山　　清代雍正年間に陸錦によって造られた涉園の黄石築山が残されたものと考えられている。

黄石假山　　黄石假山被认为是清代雍正年间陆锦所建涉园的遗迹。

yellow-stone rockery, regarded as a historic site of Sheyuan Garden built by Lu Jin, dated back to between 1723 and 1735 in the Qing Dynasty

築山上部
假山上部
top of the yellow-stone rockery

山洞内外景
山洞内外景
inside and outside views of a cave in the yellow-stone rockery

築山上の鋪地　築山中に、このような平らな鋪地空間があるのは非常に珍しい。
假山上的铺地　在假山上筑有这样平坦的铺地空间是极为稀罕的。
pavement on the top of the rockery, an even and spacious pavement on the top of the rare rockery place of its kind in rockery-designing

邃谷と山道
邃谷和山路
Deep Valley and its trail

黄石築山北側
黄石假山北侧
north to the yellow-stone rockery

黄石築山西側　　黄石の築山中には目立たないように南側の園に続く回遊路が設けられている。
黄石假山西侧　　在黄石假山中造有一条不引人注目的通向南部庭园的环游路径。
west to the yellow-stone rockery, a winding trail to the south courtyard unnoticeably lying amid the yellow-stone rockery

藤花舫　　藤花舫は陸上にある舟形の亭で、主に「旱船」と言い、別名を「不繋舟」とも言う。

藤花舫　　藤花舫是在陆地的一个舟形亭，一般称为“旱船”，别名也叫“不系舟”。

Wistaria Deocorated Land Boat, a boat-shaped pavilion, generally called “land boat”, also named “untied boat”

藤花舫内景と廊の花窓
藤花舫内景和走廊的花窗
inside view of the Wistaria Deocorated Land Boat and lattice-framed windows in the corridor

藤花舫の妻飾り

藤花舫山墙上部塑像

sculpture decoration on the upper wall of the Wistaria Deocorated Land Boat

吉祥瓦
吉祥瓦
tiles deigned with good luck symbols

鳳凰と獅子の塑像
凤凰和狮子的塑像
sculpture decorations of phoenix and lion

城曲草堂と雙照楼　　当園の建築は穏やかな屋根反りを持つものが多く、ここには揚州建築との共通点が見られる。

城曲草堂和双照楼　　在耦园建筑中，有很多造型平缓的屋檐，从中可以看到其与扬州建筑的共同点。

Thatched Cottage at the City Corner and Sun and Moon Tower, many buildings in the garden designed with gently-sloped roof, similar to the architectural style in the gardens of Yangzhou City

城曲草堂正面
城曲草堂正面
front view of the Thatched Cottage at the City Corner

城曲草堂内景
城曲草堂内景
inside view of the Thatched Cottage at the City Corner

「補讀旧書楼」扁額と「城曲草堂」扁額

“补读旧书楼”和“城曲草堂”的匾额

plaque (up): Books Re-Read Tower (Library Tower)　　plaque (down): Thatched Cottage at the City Corner

芭蕉と廊と安楽国内景
芭蕉和走廊及安乐国内景
plantain, corridor, and inside view of the Paradise Room

雙照楼と望月亭
双照楼和望月亭
Sun and Moon Tower and Moon Yearning Pavilion

雙照楼内景
双照楼内景
inside view of the Sun and Moon Tower

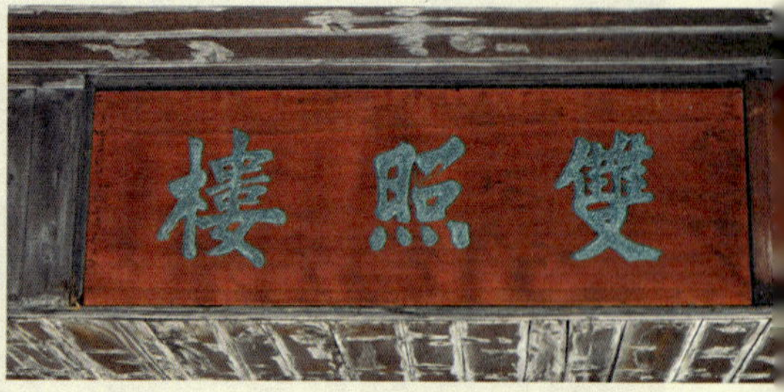

雙照楼楼上俯瞰及び扁額
双照楼俯视景及匾额
top view of the Sun and Moon Tower and its plaque

還研齋
还研斋
Returning-to-the-Inkslab House

木彫三種
三种木雕
three kinds of wood-carving

鳳凰の塑像
飞檐上凤凰的塑像
sculpture decoration of phoenix on the overhanging eave

望月亭
望月亭
Moon Yearning Pavilion

池の景観
池景
a scene of the pool

無俗韻軒
无俗韻轩
Balcony of No Frippery

無俗韻軒内景
无俗韻轩内景
inside view of Balcony of No Frippery

「枕波雙隱」磚額　　磚造りの美しい壁面装飾。左右にある磚額は対聯と同じ意図を持っている。中央の花窓との調和もすばらしい。

“枕波双隐”砖额　　一种砖造的非常漂亮的壁面装饰。左右的砖额起到对联的作用。它与中间花窗的和谐一致也非常出色。

the overhead brick plaque of Hermit Couple's Rest by Waves Beside, a kind of wall decoration with impressive brick carvings, the left and right brick plaques serving as the traditional Chinese handwriting couplet in great harmony with the lattice-framed window in the middle

無俗韻軒北庭院　東花園の西にある庭院は変化を見せて､太湖石の造形とされている。ここには西花園の景につなぐ意図が感じられる。

无俗韵轩北院　位于东花园西侧的庭园是一种为了让人看到有所变化的太湖石的造型,从中可以使人联想到西花园的景观。

north courtyard to the Balcony of No Frippery, located in the west yard of the East Garden, dotted purposefully with diversely-shaped Taihu Lake rocks, in association with the scenery appreciation of the West Garden

屋根飾り

飞檐造型

design of overhanging eave

群賢堂と鋪地
群贤堂和铺地
House of Sages and its courtyard pavement

群賢堂庭院
群贤堂庭院
courtyard of House of Sages

中園

中园

Central Garden

門庁
门厅
first gate hall

轎庁
轿厅
sedan-chair hall

載酒堂内景　　載酒堂は最も重要な客間であり、ここで客に酒をふるまう意味を持っている。

载酒堂内景　　载酒堂是一间很重要的客厅，有在此请客喝酒之意。

inside view of the Carrying Wine Hall, the most important reception hall, literally meaning a place for dining and drinking with friends

「載酒」磚額と「問字」磚額と磚門
“载酒”和“问字”的砖额及砖门
brick plaque (up): carrying wine　brick plaque (down): exploring books　the brick doorframe

楼庁(花庁)　楼庁は最も北にある二層の楼で、ここには中央に主人夫妻の部屋がある。
上層は他の女性(妾)達の部屋とされていた。完全なる私的空間であり、「女房」の別名もある。
楼厅(花厅)　楼厅是位于最北面的二层楼建筑。一楼中央是夫妻房。二楼是其他女性的房间，是完全的私密空间，名叫"女厅"。
a two-story building located in the far north-end of the garden, with the main room in the center of the first floor for the husband and wife, while the rooms on the second floor for the other female family members, a dwelling place for intimacy and privacy, also known as "the female building"

磚門

砖门

brick doorframe

西花園

西花园

West Garden

織簾老屋

织簾老屋

the Old House with Woven Curtains

織簾老屋内景と扁額と花窓
织簾老屋内景、匾额和花窗
inside view of the Old House with Woven Curtains, its plaque and lattice-framed window

太湖石と山茶花

太湖石和山茶花

Taihu Lake stones and camellia

藏書楼　　園は織簾老屋の北庭である。鋪地中にある老井が、よき点景になっている一例と言えよう。

藏书楼　　这是织簾老屋的北院，铺地中的老井可以说是一例很好的点睛之作。

Library Tower, an ancient well dotted in the north courtyard of the Old House with Woven Curtains, as the highlight of the whole scene

铺地と古井户
铺地和老井
pavement and ancient well

太湖石築山　　織簾老屋の南にある太湖石の築山。東花園が黄石の景を主にとしているのに対して、西花園はすべて太湖石を用いている。

太湖石假山　　这是在织簾老屋南侧的太湖石的假山，与东花园以黄石为主景相对比，西花园用的却都是太湖石。

Taihu-Lake-Stone Rockery, rockery heaped with Taihu Lake stones south to the Old House with Woven Curtains, in contrast to the rockery in the East Garden with yellow stones

鹤壽亭
鹤寿亭
Longevity as Crane Pavilion

漏窓と廊と空窓　屈曲する廊には、大きな空窓があり、それぞれの窓から景色の変化を楽しむことができる。

漏窗走廊和空窗　在弯弯曲曲的走廊上有很多很大的空窗，可以通过各个不同的空窗欣赏到景色的变化。

lattice-framed window, corridor and window frames, beautiful scenes varying from different perspectives through the window frames alongside the winding corridor

長方亭附近と長方亭花窓
长方亭附近及其花窗
yard nearby the Square Pavilion and its lattice-framed window

太湖石と洞門

太湖石築石の南にある塀の景観。塀中には東西二つの洞門があり、ここから入ると築山内を巡ることができる。

太湖石和洞门

这是太湖石假山南侧的墙景。在墙上,东西两侧各有一个洞门,从洞门进去可在假山内兜走。

Taihu Lake stones and doorframes,

a scene of the wall south of the Taihu-Lake-Stone Rockery, with two doorframes (east and west respectively) both accessible to a tour around the rockery

外觀

外观

Outside View

南部外觀

耦园南侧外观

outside view（from south）of the Couple's Retreat Garden

聴櫓楼の眺め

眺望听橹楼

distant view of the Listening to Sculling Boats Tower

外観水景　　当園は東、南、北が水に囲まれており、水の蘇州と言われる雰囲気を最もよく残している。

外观之水景　　该园东、南、北三面环水，很好地保留着被称为“水的苏州”的这种气氛。

watery scene outside the garden, the essence of Suzhou—a “Watery Land”,

is well-preserved in the location of the garden surrounded by a river from three sides (except west)